Original title:
Searching for Purpose and Missing My Train

Copyright © 2025 Creative Arts Management OÜ
All rights reserved.

Author: William Hawthorne
ISBN HARDBACK: 978-1-80566-167-2
ISBN PAPERBACK: 978-1-80566-462-8

Navigating the Maze of Possibilities

Around the corner, plans collide,
I trip on dreams I can't abide.
Choices scatter like lost socks,
I chase them down, oh, what a paradox.

Maps are scribbled, paths unsure,
I'm lost in thought, but that's for sure.
A train approaches, wait, don't shout!
Is this the one? Or is it out?

Clocks in the Waiting Room of Life

Tick-tock echoes in a dull despair,
The clock's a joker in a game unfair.
One minute feels like an hour's slow tease,
I play a tune on my toes, with some squeezy cheese.

The seats are empty, like my deep thoughts,
Half a sandwich and a bunch of knots.
Time crawls by, and so does my lunch,
I start a dance to avoid the crunch.

Wind Whispers on Abandoned Platforms

The wind is giggling, or so it seems,
As I reminisce about my wildest dreams.
Dusty benches hold secrets so old,
I ask them questions that never get told.

A gust of laughter sweeps through my mind,
While pigeons are pondering how to be kind.
Their coos sound like a train's distant call,
I misread my ticket, oh, who knew I'd fall?

Faded Stops Along the Way

Each stop is marked with forgotten flair,
Like a kid's drawing that's lost its dare.
I can't recall where I wanted to go,
I wave at a bus, or was that a crow?

A signpost points in ambiguous jest,
I follow on, determined to quest.
With every moment I fumble and weave,
Life's a carnival—so silly, I believe.

Waiting for a Signal of Meaning

A sign's been hiding, just out of sight,
I missed the last one, now I wait for light.
My sandwich is soggy, the pigeons look bright,
I ponder my choices as day turns to night.

I check my watch thrice, is it time yet to go?
Those lines on the board seem to put on a show.
The coffee's run cold, but my thoughts flow like dough,
It's chaos in here, yet I'm just in the flow.

A Ticket to the Unknown

My ticket's all crumpled, a mystery ticket,
Unravel its secrets, oh what a trick it.
The platform's a circus, I'm ready to pick it,
But what's my destination? A path that's quite slick it.

In line for the train, my mind starts to roam,
Where am I headed? Is it green grass or foam?
The guy in front grins, says, 'Welcome to home!',
I chuckle and wave, wondering if I'm alone.

Reflections on an Abandoned Path

Each step on this road feels oddly bizarre,
I tripped on my thoughts, now I'm lost by a car.
The signpost is broken, can't see very far,
Do I wander in circles or aim for a star?

I ask a bright squirrel if he knows the way,
He twitches and darts, then runs off to play.
I'm left with a giggle and a mind filled with gray,
Is this my adventure, or just a cliché?

The Clock's Relentless Tick

The clock's like a drummer, just marching away,
While my brain plays a tune, oh why must it sway?
Each tick is a jab, like a game that won't stay,
I ponder my choices, oh what a display!

Time's racing ahead, while I'm here in my seat,
Eating my fries and treating time as a treat.
Yet when I do rise, will I be on my feet?
Or stuck in this limbo, will I taste the defeat?

Echoes of Unfinished Dreams

I woke up late, my map's a joke,
The coffee's cold, my plans went broke.
A squirrel mocks my frantic dance,
While I forget my train of chance.

The clock ticks loud, it laughs at me,
I grab my bag, oh where's the key?
A pigeon coos as if it knows,
I'm lost in life, where purpose goes.

When the Whistle Blows Too Soon

The whistle blew, I tripped on air,
My sandwich flies, a mid-flight snare.
I waved goodbye to hopes in vain,
As I stood still like a mental grain.

'Is this the track?' I asked the cat,
She licked her paw, and sat like that.
I missed the train, the city's snore,
With dreams deferred, I look for more.

Footsteps towards a Fading Horizon

Each step I take, the ground retreats,
Like shoes on sale, my soul repeats.
Is this the path? Or just a prank?
With every stride, my thoughts all sank.

The sun sets low, a warm embrace,
While I debate my life's big race.
A dog walks by with serious flair,
Reminding me, I just don't care.

Chasing Shadows of Intent

I dream of goals, but trip on grass,
A shadow laughs, it's quite the sass.
With every turn, the world feels bright,
But my direction's just a flight.

I see my train, it's pulling away,
Leaving me lost in this comical play.
A giraffe waves, it's quite absurd,
While I wander, still undeterred.

Timekeepers of the Heart

They say time's a fickle friend,
But I've lost track, around the bend.
With clocks that dance and tick-tock play,
I missed my ride—it paused for sway.

Now life is filled with missed connections,
Like love letters that need corrections.
I chase shadows, run in vain,
While laughter echoes on the train.

Navigating Through Uncertainty

Doodle maps with crayons bright,
Lead to places out of sight.
My compass spins, oh what a thrill,
I'm lost, but hey, it's quite the chill!

With snacks in hand and style unmatched,
I wander routes that seem quite patched.
Plans written down in messy scrawl,
Yet every turn just makes me fall.

The Train That Never Came

A whistle blew, the platform shook,
But my train's a ghost, just like a book.
I waved goodbye to empty air,
As laughter broke the quiet stare.

With hotdogs served by mime-like hosts,
I chewed my thoughts, a merry boast.
Each missed ride became a tale,
Of joy found in a clumsy trail.

Unraveled Threads of Ambition

I knitted plans with dreams so bright,
But they unraveled overnight.
My sweater's still hanging by one thread,
While I chase socks beneath the bed.

Ambition's maze is quite a laugh,
I tripped on goals, but found the path.
With every twist, I learned to sway,
And dance my way through disarray.

Alone with the Departure Bell

The digital clock blinks, it shouts,
Yet here I stand, filled with doubts.
The train has left, my coffee's cold,
  I ponder plans that I can't hold.

A pigeon coos, a ticket's torn,
My phone buzzes with a brand new scorn.
Is this the day my big dreams fly?
Or just a chance to wave goodbye?

With every chime, ideas swarm,
Perhaps the chaos is the norm.
A hot dog cart rolls into view,
Maybe I'll start a food review.

I watch the sparks of trains that zoom,
While I sit here in my waiting room.
Did I forget to check the times?
At least I'm spinning silly rhymes.

The Map to Nowhere

I unfurl a map, it flips and flops,
Giggling, I trace the dotted stops.
Where's the end? Where's the start?
This paper's spun, it's witchcraft art.

I take a stroll to a hidden nook,
Maybe luck's found in a silly book.
Who needs a goal when you can roam?
Each corner can become a home.

The sun beats down, I start to sweat,
Yet each wrong turn's a fun vignette.
A picnic here? Or perhaps a dance?
Life's little mess is my best chance.

With every twist, my grin will grow,
The world's a stage, put on a show.
Next destination? Who can tell!
Adventure's just a wink and yell.

Counting Seconds on the Platform

One, two, three, the seconds tick,
My watch just broke, what a neat trick.
People rush past, they wave goodbye,
While I just stand and wonder why.

The bench seems comfy, the sun is bright,
I think I'll stay to enjoy the flight.
A lady laughs, she drops her snack,
We both just smile; there's no going back.

The loudspeaker crackles with a jest,
I've made a friend in this train-less quest.
We swap our tales of missed connections,
And ponder if life needs more direction.

So here I count, without a care,
These moments bright, a brief souvenir.
Every pause feels like a gift,
In this grand scene, I find my lift.

When Journeys Veer Off Course

The train pulled out, but I was late,
Stuck behind someone with a lot of weight.
They blocked my view of the fast train's glee,
But I found a spot to sip my tea.

A busker plays a tune so fine,
And suddenly, my worries decline.
With every chord, a laugh I find,
This twist of fate feels quite aligned.

I join the crowd, we laugh and cheer,
Who knew delays could bring such beer?
Instead of stress, there's music's call,
The joy of life outweighs it all.

So here I sway, on the sideline's edge,
While trains move fast, I'm on a ledge.
The journey's aim, it seems unclear,
But sometimes joy is simply near.

The Sound of Distant Whistles

Chasing shadows in the haze,
My feet tap dance in a daze.
I blink, I stretch, I try to see,
But trains just wave and flee from me.

The clock it laughs, I twist and shout,
Which way is up? I've lost my route!
A sausage dog runs on the track,
He looks more sure, I've lost my knack.

Each whistle blows like a cruel joke,
While I'm the punchline, feeling broke.
A sandwich dropped, a shoe untied,
I grin as I trip...with pride!

A conductor shouts, "Get on this ride!"
But I'm too busy trying to hide.
Life's a train where I can't get on,
I'll just wave my hands and yawn!

In the Land of Faded Timetables

A paper map that's lost its charm,
With every turn, I raise alarm.
"Is this the stop? Or just a stop?"
I laugh, I wave, then make a flop.

I meet a cat who claims to know,
He sprawls on tracks, completely slow.
With whiskers twitching, he takes a nap,
While I'm still fumbling with this map.

A woman shouts, "The train's gone fast!"
I scratch my head, "Can I still bask?"
The pigeons plot, they join my game,
And I just mutter "What a shame!"

In this odd world of zigzagged paths,
I hug my dreams, I share my laughs.
Timetables fade like dreams in light,
But at least I'm not alone tonight!

When the Echoes Fade

I stand and wait, don't want to budge,
Past the big sign that seems to judge.
Each echo of hope turns thick like mist,
As I search for trains that don't exist.

My coffee spills, my shoes untied,
I giggle softly, what a ride.
The only crowd is a squirrel troop,
They seem to know, while I still droop.

The whistle sounds, but it's just my phone,
"Come on!" I shout, "Don't leave me alone!"
A bee buzzes past, with greater aim,
While I stand here, feeling quite lame.

Yet laughter bubbles; I won't despair,
With funny hats and a vibrant flair.
Each misstep taken leads to a grin,
In this wacky dance, I find my win!

Lost Between Departures

On a platform where no one stays,
I check my watch in silly ways.
With coffee cups that sing and sway,
I juggle dreams like kids at play.

I dance in circles, my outfit bright,
A sock with stripes in the afternoon light.
The ticket booth is my greatest foe,
It eats my coins; where did they go?

A family of ducks waddle through the scene,
They quack their wisdom, all so keen.
With every missed train, I wear a grin,
Like life's a joke that I'm laughing in.

So here I stand—what could be worse?
Between every exit, and in every verse.
I'll wave goodbye to the trains I miss,
In this comedy, I find my bliss!

Railcards of Redemption and Reflection

I bought a ticket, quite profound,
But forgot the time, my train uncrowned.
With snacks in hand, I missed my ride,
And here I sit, the world outside.

A platform where I did not belong,
The whistle blew, the train moved on.
I waved goodbye, a cheerful flop,
In search of joy, I never stop.

Old railcards telling tales of woe,
Every line a laugh, like a stand-up show.
I wonder if the train knows my plight,
As I wait and ponder, in morning light.

Redemption's journey may be absurd,
A quirky tale that seems unheard.
But life's a ride with ups and downs,
Just keep your snacks and lose the frowns.

The Space Between Arrival and Departure

Between the stops, I lose my way,
Counting minutes, wasting the day.
A coffee spill, a sandwich dive,
In this limbo, I feel alive.

A grin from the tickets, they tease my fate,
As I check my watch, I still wait.
The clock ticks loud, the crowd moves fast,
But here I am, stuck like a cast.

In this waiting room, I have a plan,
To spot the quirky, unique, and grand.
A lady sings with a plastic ukulele,
And a kid laughs loud, it feels like a melee.

So here I lounge with folks like me,
All looking lost but wild and free.
With a chuckle shared, in this odd fest,
We might just find our own little quest.

A Map Without a Destination

Folded paper, a mess in hand,
With doodles bright, not quite as planned.
No route mapped out, just trails of fun,
A journey starts beneath the sun.

I squint to see where the lines may flow,
But bump into people, and we all go slow.
Each wrong turn, a laugh riot unfolds,
In this maze of life, there's joy to hold.

The compass spins, like a top on a rise,
And laughter erupts beneath the skies.
For every wrong, there's a right in sight,
In wanderings carefree, we own the night.

With every detour comedy strikes,
As my map confuses trains and bikes.
Adventure waits, with a wink and a grin,
Missing the train means the fun can begin.

Explorations in the Interstice

In the gaps between fate's cruel games,
I find odd things with curious names.
Like shoes untied and umbrellas bent,
In this limbo, time is well spent.

I watch the clocks spin in a daze,
While pigeons strut with a sassy gaze.
The train arrives, and I am still here,
Laughing at chaos, clapping in cheer.

A napkin sketches my next big break,
As choices swirl like a fast-paced shake.
A dance of missed trains, not stress, just glee,
In this interstice, I feel so free.

So if you find your journey deter,
Join the fun, let laughter confer.
With every chance taken, the funny remains,
In these explorations, joy never wanes.

Unwritten Chapters on the Rails

In a hurry, I left my muse,
The train departs, but I refuse.
With snacks in hand and socks askew,
I forge ahead, my thoughts askew.

Rushing past the sleep-deprived,
Wondering why my plans have thrived.
The little old man with tales so bold,
Tells me to find my treasure untold.

A ticket stub that leads astray,
Old memories in a lost bouquet.
I whistle tunes of whimsical fate,
While the train rolls off, oh what a fate!

Chapters unwritten, the plot unclear,
In this mad sprint, I'll take a beer.
Life's a journey, but where's the gain?
Waiting for my ride down the lane.

A Station Between Dreams and Reality

At a station where thoughts collide,
My dreams left early, but I still bide.
Waving goodbye to plans once grand,
The next train's late, oh isn't it grand?

Lost in a map with no clear signs,
A squirrel laughs as it steals my fries.
In a daydream, I meet the queen,
She flicks her crown, I spill caffeine.

Tickets scattered like scattered dreams,
I chase the echoes, or so it seems.
A magician's hat, where's my next chance?
Will I leap into the unknown dance?

Conductor yells, but I just grin,
Life's a carnival, let the fun begin!
I'll ride the rails, not knowing the score,
Between the dreams that I adore.

Transit Lounge of the Soul

In the lounge, I tap my feet,
A schedule lost, it's quite the feat.
With a coffee cup as my throne,
I ponder why I'm all alone.

The clock laughs, tick-tock snickers,
While I confess to bagel lickers.
A mime in the corner steals the show,
As I wonder where I did go.

Chasing after the phantom train,
Grabbing jokes in the pouring rain.
My phone buzzes, text from my cat,
"Where's my dinner? About that..."

But here I sit, a soul on pause,
Finding humor in life's little flaws.
All aboard for a ride unseen,
Just me and my thoughts, a silly routine.

The Unclaimed Luggage of Ambition

Suitcases piled like all my dreams,
Lost in the shuffle of life's loud screams.
I search for meaning through rolling bags,
While nutty squirrels dance with rags.

At baggage claim, a note I find,
"Where's the meaning? Your dreams unwind."
They say ambition's just a train ride,
But I missed the stop, I'm full of pride.

A shoe from Paris, a hat from Spain,
I wear them proud, but still feel plain.
With giggles echoing through the air,
Life's a circus, am I still there?

So here I stand with lost attire,
Riding a wave of absurd desire.
Through mismatched socks and quirky defeat,
I'll claim my luggage and take a seat.

A Path Woven with Missed Opportunities

Chasing after dreams like a cat on a spree,
But all I find are socks and an old cup of tea.
Plans made in the morning, where did they go?
I tripped on a shoelace and now I'm so slow.

Missed the bus, missed the train, what can I say?
I waved goodbye while munching my parfait.
Is it a sign or just sheer bad luck?
A goofy dance to the beat of my muck.

The compass spins wildly, like a top in my head,
Maps turned to artwork as I lie in my bed.
With each silly turn, I lose track of the hour,
It's a comedy show where I hold all the power.

Yet through all the chaos, I laugh and I twirl,
In a world of mishaps, I find a new pearl.
Life's a funny journey on a whimsical track,
With socks for my shoes, there's no turning back.

Soliloquy of the Wayward Traveler

I hopped on the wrong train, oh what a delight,
The snack car's the only thing feeling just right.
With every station missed, my heart does a flip,
"Oh, I wanted Paris, not this funny trip!"

Conversations with pigeons in a bustling square,
They give me advice, though they haven't a care.
I laugh at my fortune, it really is grand,
Who needs an agenda when chaos is planned?

Sorting my thoughts like they're puzzle pieces rare,
I find a lost ticket and inhale the fresh air.
The conductor just chuckles, he knows where I roam,
In a land full of sidetracks, I still feel at home.

So here's to the journeys, where maps just derailed,
With fanciful detours, my spirit unveiled.
Each oversight's a treasure, a whimsical boon,
Laughing at life, I make my own tune.

The Tides of Time On the Tracks

Rushing to nowhere like leaves in a breeze,
Each moment elusive, just like a tease.
I thought I was early, but turns out I'm late,
Balancing muffins while juggling my fate.

Oh, the platform is empty, just shadows and sighs,
A ticket in hand, I'm a man on the rise.
But every departure feels stuck in a loop,
As I folk-dance with squirrels, a motley troop.

So what if I wander, I'll twirl through the fog,
With a suitcase of dreams and my old trusty dog.
Counting my blessings like train cars that flow,
It's hard to feel lost when you're part of the show.

The clock keeps on ticking, but laughter won't fade,
In this circus of time, I'm so glad I stayed.
For missed connections hold stories untold,
And I'll wear my blunders like glittering gold.

Unlocked Gates in a Train Station of Dreams

There's magic in transit, where time goes to play,
With doors that keep opening and leading astray.
I search for my route, through tunnels and haze,
But really, it's more like a surreal maze.

Platform shoes on, I'm the star of the show,
Strutting my stuff where the lost travelers go.
Every oncoming train is a beckoning light,
But I fumble my ticket, now that's quite a plight!

Clouds of confusion, yet I find joy in jest,
Each delay is a chance for a comical quest.
With a wink and a grin, I embrace the tease,
As I dance with the raindrops, it's all a breeze.

So here I will linger, by the gates left ajar,
With dreams in my pocket, life's a quirky bazaar.
Every missed connection a story to keep,
In this station of whimsy, I drift off to sleep.

Journeys That Lead to Nowhere

I woke up late, oh what a sight,
The train had left, I missed my flight.
In pajamas, I start to stroll,
With coffee breath, I lose control.

I chase the tracks, but ducks are fowl,
They quack and honk, they laugh, and howl.
I wave my arms, it's quite absurd,
But laughter echoes, louder than words.

A squirrel gives me a funny glance,
As I attempt my frantic dance.
The bus is here, but I'm so slow,
I guess it's time to just let go.

Each missed chance is a little prank,
Life's a ride on a shady plank.
So if you see me running late,
Just know I'm having fun with fate.

Unfolding Destinies Along the Tracks

I bought a ticket, took a seat,
But oh dear, there's still defeat!
My train's gone zooming, engine loud,
And I'm left here, in a crowd.

With every platform I survey,
I spot more folks with trains at bay.
They cheer and clap, they wave goodbye,
While I just munch my stale french fry.

A mime appears and steals my show,
Pretending to push, I kick in tow.
And through his antics, I can see,
A moment's pause, just let it be.

The schedule's chaos makes me smile,
I'll take my time; I'll stay awhile.
On this wild ride of missed delight,
I'll embrace the day, it feels just right.

The Weight of a Missed Connection

The whistle blew, the doors all closed,
And here I stand, oft discomposed.
With suitcase heavy, full of fluff,
My plans unraveled, isn't that tough?

A pigeon struts, he looks just fine,
While I'm bemoaning lost design.
He's got his bread, and here I fuss,
His life's a breeze, mine's chaotic plus.

Each moment ticking, feels like lead,
As I ponder where I should tread.
But laughter bubbles, brings me cheer,
Maybe I'd rather linger here.

So here's to the ones who miss it all,
We find our way, even when we fall.
With humor's glint, through ups and downs,
We craft our tales, without those frowns.

Contemplations at the Crossover

I sit and watch the trains assemble,
Each one a dream that's gone to tremble.
The lights are flashing, time to go,
While I, confused, have lost the flow.

A toddler giggles on the floor,
Her lunch spills out, a veggie war.
I chuckle loud, joy shared and clear,
While missing trains are held so dear.

The clock is ticking, but what's the rush?
With life's own beat, I'm here in hush.
If fate means waiting on the track,
I'll take my time, I won't look back.

As crowds disperse and sunsets glow,
I'll wave goodbye to trains I know.
In life's grand scheme, it's just a tease,
But I'll embrace it, if you please!

The Elusive Next Stop

I stand on the platform, looking around,
Wondering if my thoughts should make a sound.
The train zooms by, but I miss the call,
Like chasing rainbows, I trip and fall.

With ticket in pocket, yet no train in sight,
I wave goodbye to my chances, polite.
A conductor laughs as he whispers my fate,
While I juggle my bags and contemplate.

The schedule's a puzzle, a game with no clues,
As I search for a ride, I ponder my views.
Is this just a pit stop in life's grand ballet?
Or am I misstepping, lost in the fray?

But laughter erupts as I sit with my snack,
I may have missed one, but I'll catch the next track.
For each little stumble and each silly plight,
Brings a chuckle and joy, like stars in the night.

Tracks of Forgotten Dreams

I checked my watch, but it's stuck on a whim,
As trains whiz by, my hopes start to dim.
Last time I practiced my grand exit plan,
I missed my ride, but I still feel like a fan.

My suitcase a dancer, it sways 'round my feet,
Collecting the tales of this whimsical feat.
The signs keep on flashing, but I can't read the truth,
I need a conductor to guide my lost youth.

The crowd rushes forward, I shuffle and sway,
With dreams on the line and my ticket at bay.
Will my thoughts catch a train, or shall they deride?
Like a sardine sandwich, I have nowhere to hide.

In the end, I laugh at the delightful absurd,
For life's quirky tracks are a little blurred.
With each missed connection, a giggle's the prize,
A journey of mishaps under foggy skies.

Beyond the Horizon of Intent

I packed my intentions, so neat in a row,
But trains have their agendas that I never know.
They rocket away while I'm lost in a trance,
I guess it's a lesson in life's crazy dance.

My compass spins wildly, it dreams of the alight,
Yet I'm stuck here chuckling at my silly plight.
Should I chase every gust, or just sit and regret?
With dreams in my pocket, there's no need to fret.

The horizon is bright, but oh so far away,
I'll trade my ticket for this comical play.
With friends all around, I'll embrace my mistake,
We'll laugh at the journey, for laughter's at stake.

So here's to the trains I've missed by a mile,
Each detour's a chapter, an unplanned style.
I'll dance down this path, let the laughter unfold,
For life's little blunders are all worth their gold.

The Unseen Destination

The station is bustling, and I'm in a daze,
I thought I saw time, but it's lost in a maze.
Each sign points a different way, what gives?
Is the train to my future hiding where it lives?

I fumble and tumble, no plan in my hand,
As I chase down my thoughts, like grains of fine sand.
My boarding pass flutters like a bird in flight,
While I clumsily scramble, avoiding the night.

"Next train in five!" says a voice overhead,
As I sit on a bench, filled with dreams and dread.
Is my coffee a beacon, or just wishful steam?
I've sighted my train, but it's just in a dream.

I'll take my missteps as part of the fun,
For life's just a journey, and I've only begun.
So here's to the turns that I've made with a grin,
At the unseen destination, let the laughter begin!

In Pursuit of the Unseen

Chasing shadows on my way,
Hopscotch dreams in broad daylight.
The clock's hand spins, oh what a play,
Missed my train—what a sight!

Running fast with a silly grin,
A sandwich flies out of my bag.
People stare as I dash again,
Oh, what a train I now drag!

Laughter bubbles with every step,
A dog laughs, oh what a sight!
Who needs trains? I'll just prep,
For a bus that's not in sight!

In this jumble, bright and wild,
I find joy in the misplanned mess.
Life's a ride—let's stay child,
Catch the joy, who needs success?

Whispers of the Unraveled Map

A map unfurled but all askew,
With landmarks drawn in crayon bold.
I'm off to find a brew,
That's not the train station told!

Turn left, turn right, or maybe back,
I leap over a dog in glee.
The sound of wheels I now lack,
But there's cake—it calls to me!

Sipping coffee in the sun,
"Where's the train?" I chuckle light.
Let's savor this, we're on the run,
Exploring what feels just right!

Maps are guides to nowhere near,
With crumpled edges and odd roads.
I'll wander here without a fear,
For adventure, it easily goads.

The Silence After the Last Call

A bell rings out, and I just stare,
The echo's gone, the crowd has fled.
I shrug it off without a care,
Is there pie? Oh, I just bled!

In this silence, I find a creed,
Messy food and laughter soar.
No train in sight, who's got the need?
Taco truck? Please, more and more!

People mock my feigned despair,
"Is the train lost?" they jest in cheer.
With a grin, I toss my hair,
"Let's eat cake—who needs a steer?"

In this stillness, life unfolds,
With laughter loud and appetite.
Once the train's lost, joy molds,
It's a feast with every bite!

Layovers of Reflection

Waiting here, my feet a dance,
A suitcase spins, oh what a show!
Life's a chance, let's take a glance,
 Did I miss my train? Oh no, no!

With snack-filled bags and daring schemes,
 My heart beats in a polka tune.
 Who needs a train when joy redeems?
 Let's wait together, a fun commune!

On this platform, I take a seat,
Next to thoughts of trip and snack.
With every bite, life tastes so sweet,
Forget the train, we won't look back.

In this layover, time expands,
A world unfolds in every crumb.
I'm flicking paper, tossing strands,
 Finding purpose? Yes, let's hum!

All Aboard the Uncharted Adventure

I left my house with great delight,
With coffee hot and spirits bright.
But oh, the platform came and went,
I waved goodbye—my train exempt.

A ticket clutched, my dreams in tow,
I sniffed the air for joy to grow.
Instead, I found just pigeons there,
Who seemed to giggle without care.

I chased a scrap of paper fluttering,
Thinking it held my destiny's uttering.
But it just led to a runaway kite,
So off I went, just feeling light.

With feet on tracks and heart on fire,
I wondered if this was my desire.
While trains sped past in a blur of steel,
I found the comedy of the unreal.

In Transit with Unanswered Questions

I boarded late, the doors all closed,
I sighed deeply, my mind was dozed.
Where was I headed? Who could say?
These signs just laugh and fade away.

The lady next to me knit with glee,
While I fretted on my misspent spree.
"Excuse me, ma'am, is this the right track?"
She smiled wide and let out a clack.

I inspected my map, upside down,
Wondering if I'd reach the town.
But everyone else seemed quite upbeat,
While I debated with my own two feet.

As stations passed, my focus drifted,
Thoughts raced on like trains that shifted.
When the conductor said we'd arrived,
I just shrugged—adventure contrived.

Crossroads of the Heart's Journey

Two paths diverged, I stood and stared,
A map in hand, my vision impaired.
One way was smooth, the other a mess,
I chose the wrong one, I must confess.

I walked in circles, like a lost mime,
Thinking about my wasted time.
The station clock laughed, hands on its face,
And I did a jig, mixed feelings in place.

I asked the birds, "Which way to fly?"
They chirped a tune, as if to imply,
That life's grand journey's not mapped out clear,
But filled with laughter, joy, and cheer.

So here I sit, on this bustling street,
With a sandwich crammed and no train seat.
At the crossroads, I find my way,
Sharing my tale, come what may.

Rails of Resilience and Regret

The whistle blew, but I wasn't there,
I stumbled in, hair wild as a bear.
The train had left, laughter echoed loud,
I danced on the platform, feeling proud.

With snacks in hand and a grin so wide,
I made new friends, let fate decide.
The journey's fun, I soon discovered,
As we all made plans and snacks were covered.

Regret took a back seat on this ride,
I learned to laugh, and not just glide.
For life's a track with twists and bends,
And sometimes missing trains just makes new friends.

So here's to those who stray from the route,
With stories to share and bits to shout.
In every delay, a secret gem,
And laughs to share, we ride again.

Waiting for the Dawn at Midnight Station

At the station under moon's glow,
I ponder where the next train will go.
A clock ticks slow, the night is long,
I hum a tune that feels all wrong.

A squirrel steals my cheese on a whim,
As I sit with dreams that start to dim.
The ticket man gives me a grin,
While I wonder when the fun begins.

A fellow waits with mismatched socks,
He counts the stars like ticking clocks.
I spill my coffee, oh what a mess,
Laughing at fate's absurd jest.

The night drags on, it starts to break,
Not sure if it's dreams I should make.
With each train that passes by,
I wave goodbye with a hopeful sigh.

The Long Pause Between Heartbeats

In the silence where seconds freeze,
I ponder if it's all just a tease.
With popcorn dreams stuck in my head,
I laugh at the plans I never fed.

The universe spins while I'm stuck still,
Counting fish in an imaginary mill.
A bird swoops down, makes a mess,
As I sit here feeling the stress.

I spot a shoe that's lost its mate,
Wondering if it's sealed my fate.
A nearby cat strikes a noble pose,
And I'm here pondering my next prose.

Each heartbeat echoes like a drum,
Am I awake or just feeling numb?
I talk to clouds, they mock my plight,
Oh, what a laugh in the dead of night!

Inked on the Pages of Time

They say life's ink can easily smudge,
Yet here I sit, feeling the grudge.
With blank pages waiting, hope in bloom,
I trip over words spelling my doom.

A pencil rolls off, takes a dive,
While thoughts swim round, barely alive.
I find joy in a coffee stain,
Like a map to where I can't explain.

Each line I write, a comic twist,
In the script of life that I can't resist.
Absurdities bundled in rhymes I weave,
I chuckle at plans time did not leave.

The clock's hands race, a comic chase,
As I ponder what went out of place.
My notebook laughs as I miss a chance,
In this wacky, fate-filled dance.

Farewell to Unfulfilled Plans

With a suitcase full of missed trains,
I wave goodbye to joyful gains.
Plans crumpled like a paper kite,
I laugh at dreams, oh what a sight!

A map's all wrinkled, Friday's guest,
Ticking clocks put my patience to test.
I climb on thoughts like they're high hills,
Chasing moments that gave me thrills.

The boldest idea slips through my grip,
Like a pirate ship on a caffeine trip.
I flip through memos that never grew,
Finding humor in the "what ifs" too.

So here I am, with goofy plans,
Counting blessings in rubbled cans.
Cheers to dreams that went astray,
I'll find the joy in this funny play!

A Composition of Silent Tracks

I looked left, I looked right,
The train has left my line of sight.
With coffee in hand, I stand still,
Reflecting on dreams, what a thrill!

The station clock ticks, oh so slow,
I debate if I should stay or go.
In the distance, I hear a light chime,
Was it my stop? Oh, what a crime!

Passengers rush, like ants on the run,
While I sip my brew, I'm not yet done.
Life's a journey, so they say,
But I missed that train—what a day!

So I'll wander here, take a detour,
Laugh at the chaos, that's for sure.
With every delay, comes a funny tale,
Maybe a train, if I don't bail.

Unraveled Lines in the Map of Life

The map I hold is a jigsaw piece,
With lines so squiggly, I can't find peace.
Every station seems to play a joke,
"Next stop is fun!"—the conductor spoke.

With messy hair and mismatched shoes,
I dance like no one cares, I muse.
To find direction feels like a test,
But let's just grin—it's for the best!

So many trains, yet I stand still,
Munching snacks, collecting a thrill.
Laughter echoes in the waiting hall,
"Did you miss that train?" I'll just stall.

Here's to the journey, quirky and bright,
With wrong turns that lead to delight.
I'll gather stories, funny and bold,
In this winding path, I'll find my gold!

Transit Between Tomorrow and Yesterday

I missed my train but found a bench,
Where time melts, a curious wench.
Yesterday's dreams dance in the air,
Tomorrow's trains? Who knows where!

A squirrel steals crumbs from my bag,
As I crack up, he's got the swag.
His tiny feet tap on the floor,
Is he my ride? I'll wait for more!

Conversations float like clouds above,
With stories shared and laughter of love.
Time's not lost if we find the joy,
In random delays, life's but a toy.

So here I remain, on a whim,
Collecting moments, not so grim.
For missing a train is just a game,
Where fun finds its way, never the same!

The Heartbeat of Uncertainty

A tick-tock rhythm fills my ears,
As I stand here drowning in fears.
The train I've missed, like a bad pun,
Life's a ride; we just have fun!

Each beep and honk, a comic play,
As passengers rush, I want to stay.
With circus acts right by my side,
Every delay feels like a ride.

Laughter weaves through the crowded space,
I glance at faces, every race.
A spontaneous trip, why not today?
If I can't board, I'll find my way!

With peeks into trains as they roll through,
The stories that echo, fresh and new.
In this heartbeat of fun and strife,
I find my purpose, that's the spice of life!

Souvenirs from the Lost Expedition

I packed my bags in quite a rush,
But left my map - oh what a hush!
With snacks galore and hopes so bright,
I stomped my foot, it wasn't right.

The signs were wrong, the paths confused,
A penguin dance? I surely bruised.
Collecting rocks, I lost my goal,
Yet laughed so hard, it filled my soul.

A compass pointing everywhere,
I chased a squirrel — please don't despair!
My train departed, that's no lie,
But here I am - I'll just pass by.

With trinkets small from places strange,
I'll start a shop, that'll be the change!
Each quirky find, a tale to tell,
Collecting laughs — oh, I do it well.

The Miles Between Us and Dreams

Late night dreams of distant lands,
Polka-dots and marching bands.
But waking up with morning light,
I missed the bus — oh what a sight!

With mismatched socks and hair a mess,
I threw my shoes — my life's a guess.
The miles are short when you're this late,
But funny faces? That's first-rate!

A traffic jam, a guy in spandex,
He's not my type, but what the heck!
I wave, he grins, we share the road,
Together we can bear this load.

At last I find a seat to claim,
It's all a part of this strange game.
Each mile I traveled, full of schemes,
Chasing laughter, not just dreams.

A Journey Through Foggy Mindscapes

I woke up lost, my coffee's cold,
With foggy thoughts, my mind feels old.
I wander in a gentle haze,
My train's long left; I'm in a daze!

The clouds above, they tease my head,
A rubber chicken sings instead.
I giggle hard, it makes no sense,
But humor's here as my defense.

In corners dark, I find a clown,
He makes me smile, erasing frowns.
Content to float on whims of chance,
I'm swept away in laughter's dance.

As moments pass, I start to see,
The joy in chaos sets me free.
And though lost tracks make me puff,
This foggy trip is more than enough.

Renditions of a Delayed Departure

I sprinted fast, the clock's a tease,
With suitcase wheels that squeal and wheeze.
Platform five, a red balloon,
But alas, my train's left - oh the ruin!

The station's filled with quirky sights,
A juggler tossed with all his might.
I cheered him on, forgot my plight,
As laughter echoed through the night.

Checking boards with eye-drawn maps,
I just can't wait, and yet I tap.
My tune of woe plays loud and clear,
While all around folks shed a tear!

A delayed departure? Let it be,
I'll write a song, just wait and see!
For every missed train, lost in fun,
Has turned to stories — I've just begun!

On the Edge of the Rails

I stand here like a statue, quite absurd,
My thoughts are racing, but I'm still as a bird.
The clock keeps ticking, much too fast,
Where's that train? I should have passed!

People bustle past with bags and flair,
While I'm out here pretending I don't care.
A sandwich in hand, oh, what a sight,
Will I catch a train, or just be polite?

The whistle blows; I jump with surprise,
But it's just a pigeon; oh, how time flies!
I laugh at myself, it's a bit of a joke,
As I trip on my shoelace and nearly croak.

With every missed train, my dreams take flight,
I hop on laughter; it feels just right.
Who needs a journey when life is this fun?
I'll just ride the wave 'til the day is done!

The Promise of Tomorrow's Train

I daydream here, on Platform Nine,
Tomorrow's train is right on time.
But today feels stuck in a quirky zone,
Where the snacks are plenty, yet I'm all alone.

A mime walks by, making grand gestures,
Pretending to board, oh, what a disaster!
I wish I could follow, but my ticket's for later,
Would he chew my sandwich? Just need a gator!

The big board flickers, displays my plight,
My train's running late; it's quite the fright!
I check my shoes for a journey unplanned,
Two left feet might be my travel brand.

So here I'll sit with a grin on my face,
Waiting for joy, I'll make this a race.
Maybe tomorrow, this train will arrive,
And I'll end up somewhere, feeling alive!

Lost Tracks and Wandering Thoughts

My mind's on a track that's gone off the rails,
Every thought a train with no set of trails.
I wear mismatched socks, is that a crime?
Lost tracks of laughter, I simmer in time.

The station's alive with a cacophony bright,
Yet my focus is scattered, much like my sight.
It's a juggling act with my bags and my dreams,
As the train rolls by, bursting at the seams.

I wave at the conductors, they smile and nod,
But I stand here waiting, feeling quite odd.
I've missed my connection; my heart's in a crank,
Sipping on Starbucks, but using a tank!

An announcement blares, it's a whimsical tune,
Catch the next train, oh, I hum along soon.
So here's to the chaos, my rhymes and my routes,
I'll laugh through the waiting, while life's on the flouts!

The Journey Between Platforms

Between two platforms, I sip on my tea,
Trying to figure out where I should be.
Life's like a train, always pulling away,
With seats filled with strangers, what will they say?

An old lady laughs; she's wearing a hat,
Says, "Come join my journey; we'd have a chat!"
I smile and nod, but my train's long gone,
Yet here I am, with new friends to dawn.

We swap jokes and tales, the time drips away,
Why rush on a train when you could play?
And though I may miss that glamorous ride,
It's the moments of laughter where real joys abide.

So here's to the paths that we wander without haste,
Life's tracks are just circuits we each get to taste.
I'll dance on the platforms, and sing to the breeze,
And laugh at the chaos, oh, how life's a tease!

A Station of Reflection

At the platform, I stand tall,
With my luggage and dreams, feeling small.
The train whizzes by, leaves me in the dust,
I ponder my life, who knew I'd combust?

A ticket I bought, but it's not in my pocket,
My schedule's a joke, I'm both train and rocket.
An old man chuckles, his beard full of crumbs,
'You've got to run faster or buy you some drums!'

The station clock laughs, its hands play a game,
Tick-tock it grins, just fueling my shame.
The poets and dreamers, they ride without care,
While I practice my moves, in the middle of nowhere.

So here I remain, at this whimsical spot,
Where time's a quagmire, and purpose, a plot.
I'll dance with my baggage, laugh in a spin,
Maybe that's the adventure I'm meant to begin.

The Unwritten Itinerary

Maps upside down, I scratch at my head,
Plans once so clear, now scattered like bread.
The train pulls away, just a puff in the air,
I'm left with my thoughts and a glum, fuzzy stare.

A poet beside me quotes verses from life,
As I fumble for meaning, his wisdom cuts like a knife.
'It's all in the journey,' he smirks as he sips,
I mumble my thanks—while he's off on his trips.

Tickets to nowhere, are perfectly fine,
I'll ride on my dreams, aboard a wild line.
The more that I wander, the less that I plan,
Perhaps I'll find purpose, while stuck in a jam.

Each station a chapter, each stop a surprise,
I smile at the chaos, embrace the disguise.
This unwritten route leads to laughter and cheer,
Who needs a true path, when shenanigans near?

Threads of Fate Unspooled

At the station I sit, knitting life's funny threads,
With a pattern confused, tangled dreams in my head.
The trains zip right past, like time in a whirl,
While I knot my intentions, each twist makes me twirl.

A cat with a suitcase walks past with a frown,
As I mumble at fate, like a fool with a crown.
'Where's the party?' I shout, but no one replies,
Just pigeons and hitchhikers roll their small eyes.

A woman in red, her hat the size of a moon,
Teaches me laughter, in the midst of a tune.
With each clumsy yarn, I untangle the plight,
And realize the hilarity in this crazy night.

So here's to the threads that lead us astray,
As I craft a new dream with each passing day.
While fate spins its wheel and delivers a jest,
I'll knit all the journeys, and wear them with zest.

Footprints on a Dusty Platform

My footprints line up, a comical trail,
In the dust on the platform, a marksman's sale.
Step left, step right, where did my train go?
While I dance with the dust, and put on a show.

The whistle blows loudly, like a cow in a brawl,
I'm juggling my coffee, I feel quite the fool.
Maybe this is the ride that I truly must take,
A circus of moments, with each laugh to make.

A fellow beside me, a shoe on his head,
Complains about baggage or dreams underfed.
We bond over chaos, while missing our ride,
Two kings of misfortune, with laughs as our guide.

So here at the station, where moments collide,
I'll flap my arms wildly, take life in my stride.
With each passing train, I ponder and grin,
For the laughs that I gather, are the journeys I win.

The Ascent of Unfulfilled Wishes

I woke up late, what a delight,
My plans went south, a comical fright.
Socks unmatched, a fashion faux pas,
Chasing the bus, like a lost quasar.

Noodles for breakfast, a sticky affair,
I spilled sauce like I didn't care.
With each step I dodged a runaway shoe,
Life's a circus, with no clown crew.

Dreams on hold, just like my ride,
Juggling tasks, with chaos as my guide.
Missed my train, but I found a snack,
Who knew a donut would lighten the lack?

So here I stand, the clock ticks loud,
Hoping my fortune spins 'round in a crowd.
Laughter echoes in this unsure plight,
At least I'll arrive when the timing's right.

When the Compass Goes Astray

A compass spin, a map that's bent,
Wander lost, though I once was intent.
I followed the signs, but they led to tea,
Sipping Earl Grey while I forgot to flee.

GPS dead, it lost its style,
Funny how plans can go off a mile.
I asked a cat, but it just stared back,
Guess I'll be late—I'm off on a snack!

Every bus stop, a mystery profound,
Where's the right direction—lost and found?
With humor on hand, I wave goodbye,
To the train that I saw, just flash by.

But I'll make the journey, even if slow,
With breadcrumbs of laughter, where'er I go.
Turns out delight's found not in haste,
But in the moments and joys we taste.

Unread Timetables of the Heart

I glanced at the clock, oh what a surprise,
Time's a trickster in a slick disguise.
Missed the last call, it's what I do best,
Running on dreams, leaving me stressed.

The heart scribbles notes, but what's the plot?
It's in chaos—who cares if it's hot!
A love like a train, that's forever delayed,
But I make the most, in my humor parade.

Under streetlights, I dance with the night,
Each missed connection feels oddly polite.
The rhythm of laughter fills empty space,
While I search for my heart in this hurried race.

Chasing whispers of passion untold,
With giggles and snickers, for stories bold.
In unread timetables, the heart takes flight,
So here's to the chaos, my timing feels right!

Crossing Tracks of Dilemmas

The train's on the tracks with a mind of its own,
While I juggle dramas, feeling overblown.
Pigeons mock me as I run for my stop,
But I laugh at my fate, like candy that pops.

Decisions collide, like trains in the mist,
Should I take the path where I can't resist?
Or follow the signs that lead to a snack,
A sandwich or two to put me on track?

I toss a coin—tails, it's dessert!
Though life's like a circus, it sometimes can hurt.
My ticket's a joke, but I'll smile at the ride,
Finding joy in the errors, with laughter as my guide.

So here's to the choices that make us feel numb,
And the quirky adventures that all seem so fun.
In the maze of tracks, I'll find my own way,
With humor and heart, I'm alive every day.

A Train Whistle in the Distance

I woke up late, the clock did chime,
My coffee brewed, but I lost track of time.
Down the stairs, I flew in a haze,
Chasing shadows in a morning daze.

Outside the window, a smoke plume curls,
I wave goodbye like a lost little girl.
The train rolls on, its whistle a joke,
While I stand here, the world's gone up in smoke.

With my shoelaces tangled, I trip on the step,
An audience forms, oh what a misstep!
"Catch the next one," they chuckle and grin,
But my next adventure has yet to begin.

So here I remain, as trains pass me by,
With dreams in my pocket and a sigh in the sky.
A journey aborted, can't find my way,
Yet laughter erupts, what a merry ballet!

Journeys Gone Awry

Left my house with a plan so grand,
To hop on a train, oh, wasn't it planned?
But the socks I wore were two different hues,
And my favorite book? I forgot to choose.

I dashed to the station, my heart in a race,
Only to find I'd no ticket in place.
The conductor laughed, said, "You've got fine flair,
But you'll need something more, like a ticket to share!"

With pockets now empty and eyelids aglow,
I wandered the platform, much to and fro.
The pigeons took off, they'd gone for a ride,
While I waited in line, my plans had all died.

So I laughed at myself while I stood in the queue,
What else can you do when adventures are few?
But fate's got a plan; it twists and it bends,
Maybe my lost train is just making new friends!

Railmarks of a Wandering Heart

The schedule was bold, a departure at noon,
But I took my time, for I'm never immune.
With candy in hand, and shoes mismatched too,
I danced to the rhythm of a world askew.

At the rail where the tracks met, I paused for a snack,
A squirrel stole my sandwich; oh, what a hack!
I ran for my ride, but the whistle blew loud,
The train rolled away as I stood in the crowd.

With a sigh and a shrug, I leaned on a pole,
Wondering if missing was part of the goal.
The ticket I had, was a joke in disguise,
Life had its humor, with all of its highs.

Yet in every misstep, there's fun to be found,
With laughter and chatter that dances around.
Today's little blunder is tomorrow's great tale,
As I chase my own train, on this quirky old rail!

An Intermission of Lost Aspirations

I packed my dreams in a duffle bag bright,
With hopes that would shine in the morning light.
But tripped on a suitcase, my plans went astray,
Oh well, what's a fumble on a fine travel day?

I found my way here, to an empty café,
With a latte that's cold, and crumpets to sway.
Outside, the trains zoom by like a glance,
While I'm stuck inside, lost in a trance.

A good friend I met, who argued her way,
Said, "Life's just a stage, you improvise play!"
She fingered my arm, her pet hamster in tow,
"We'll write a new script if you're feeling low."

So I sat down again and I sipped my cold drink,
Turns out missing trains can inspire us to think.
With laughter the balm and snacks on my plate,
I'll miss my next train, but I'll still celebrate!

Detours of the Driven

I walked the platform, missed my ride,
Through twists and turns, what a wild slide!
I chased my coffee, spilled on my shoe,
Who knew this journey would lead to a zoo?

An advert caught my eye, shiny and bright,
Time for a snack, oh what a delight!
A burger so tall, could've been a tower,
I'll eat it now, then sprint in an hour!

A train whistled past, and I waved in glee,
No chance of catchin', but look at me!
I danced on the tracks, a sight to behold,
An unplanned encore, brave and bold!

With shoes untied and my head in a spin,
I found my way back but forgot where to begin.
Life's a crazy ride, full of twists and bends,
At least I've got my burger and funny friends!

Unmet Connections in Transit

The clock is ticking, and I'm on the roam,
Missed the last train, oh where is home?
I took a wrong turn, and now I'm in France,
Trying to fit in, but they don't dance!

A pigeon just cooed like he knows my plight,
I asked him for help, but it took flight.
An old man chuckled, pointed to the moon,
Thought maybe he'd sing me a travel tune!

With bags full of snacks, I'll see this through,
I'll make a new path, all fresh and new.
Why run for the train when you can roam free?
I'll ride on the wings of my own comedy!

A bus pulls up, and I hop on board,
Next stop's the bakery, that's the accord!
Missing my train turned into a feast,
Adventure awaits, at the very least!

The Shadows of Abandoned Itineraries

With a map in my hand and no clue in sight,
I missed my own stop — what a silly fright!
Tangled in routes that lead me astray,
But the snacks in my bag say I'm okay!

I strolled through the park, where trains made a fuss,
Saw ducks in tuxedos, all aboard the bus.
I waved to the birds, they squawked back in jest,
Who knew miscommunication could be such a quest?

A wanderer paused with a puzzled look,
Asked if my guidebook was more like a cookbook.
We laughed at our plight and shared quite a laugh,
Decided on travel — on mismatched paths!

At the end of it all, I danced with glee,
Fate led me here, and oh, how it's free!
Life's just a train ride with friends that you meet,
Next destination? A bakery treat!

Riddles Written in the Dust of Platforms

Dust on the tracks, tales left untold,
I missed my dear train, but found pirate gold!
A squirrel scampered, wearing a hat,
Prompting me to ponder — where's my mat?

I scribbled a riddle on a crumpled old fare,
"Where do lost trains go? To the land of despair?"
But clarity dawned as I munched on a fry,
Maybe they're dancing with stars in the sky!

Pigeons played chess, or at least so it seemed,
Tail feathers flashing, their egos redeemed.
I joined in the fun, played a round or two,
In the game of lost trains, who knew what was true?

As dusk softly fell and I snacked with some flair,
Maybe a missed train means life's debonair.
So here's to the journeys that twist and confound,
Riddles of joy in the laughter I found!

An Abandoned Journey's End

I packed my bags with glee and cheer,
But tripped on my laces, oh dear, oh dear!
The map in my hands was upside down,
While I waved my goodbyes in a clownish frown.

The station clock ticked a tune of despair,
As I stumbled about without a care.
It seemed like a party I wasn't in,
While trains rolled by with a smirking grin.

I chased after dreams atop a train car,
But realized I was way off, by far.
With my snacks now scattered in the breeze,
I laughed at the chaos, feeling quite at ease.

So here I stand, lost and bemused,
Amidst strangers laughing, thoroughly amused.
They'll tell the tale of my grand misfit,
The traveler who never quite made it.

Railways of Wonder and Worry

I woke up late, what a surprise,
Just in time to see trains fly by!
With shoes on wrong and hair like a mop,
I raced to my fate, but just couldn't stop.

Tickets in hand, a fumble and flop,
The line was too long, my heart started to drop.
While folks rolled their eyes and sighed in disdain,
I twirled on my heel, feeling the strain.

The platform a circus, oh what a sight!
Everyone bustling, quite a delight.
Except for me, the king of the fools,
Staring in awe as time brutally rules.

And as my train puffed away from the bay,
I pondered my skills at delay and dismay.
Perhaps I'm meant for a different track,
One where the latecomers don't hold back!

Echoes of a Forgotten Route

At dawn I arose, like a faraway bell,
Thinking of journeys—I do wish them well.
But coffee in hand, oh what a blunder,
Turns out that my pants were under my thunder!

Stumbling outside in a whirlwind of haste,
I waved to the sun, a flustered embrace.
But alas, all I saw was the red light's glare,
Wishing I was anywhere but standing there.

With each train that zipped by, I felt the pain,
Like comedic tragedy in a life's refrain.
"Get your ticket!" I hollered quite loud,
While the pigeons cooed, forming a crowd.

Then came the laugh, a chuckle from me,
For the real journey isn't just to be free.
It's to stumble and trip and embrace the absurd,
In a world full of chaos—nothing's unheard!

A Train of Thought Derailed

Thoughts racing faster than a freight train's speed,
I set off on my path, but forgot to heed.
With a tune in my head and a skip in my step,
I missed the whole point, oh what a misstep!

In line for my ticket, I suddenly froze,
As someone stepped on my favorite toes.
With laughter erupting from my own clumsy cheer,
I wondered if life's one big comedy gear.

Fumbling and mumbling, I missed my whole shot,
But I found unexpected joy in the plot.
Those little mishaps make life spin round,
Like a train that's lost but joyously bound.

So here I am, on a whimsical ride,
With hiccups and giggles my faithful guide.
Let trains come and go, I'll just join the fun,
For who needs a ticket when the laughter's begun?

www.ingramcontent.com/pod-product-compliance
Lightning Source LLC
Chambersburg PA
CBHW071844160426
43209CB00003B/409